# I'm Not Taking It Anymore

Barbara S. Corley

Kingdom Builders Publications LLC

© 2019 Barbara S. Corley
I'm Not Taking It Anymore
Kingdom Builders Publications, LLC

All rights reserved. No part of this book may be reproduced or transmitted in any form or by any means without written permission from the author.

Printed in the USA

**ISBN**
978-0-578-46289-9

**Library of Congress Control Number**
2019935915

**Authored by**
Barbara S. Corley

**Editor**
Kingdom Builders Publications
Lakisha S. Forrester

**Cover Design**
ID 12762307 © Jason Stitt | Dreamstime.com
LoMar Designs

*I'm Not Taking It Anymore*

*This book belongs to*

# CONTENTS

PREFACE .................................................................V

INTRODUCTION ..................................................... 1

FIRST INCIDENT .................................................... 4

RECONNECTING ................................................... 11

CHILD SUPPORT ................................................... 13

THE ABUSE BEGINS ............................................. 15

APPOINTMENTS................................................... 20

THREE DAYS & TWO NIGHTS................................ 25

SURGERY ............................................................. 28

FORECLOSURE .................................................... 33

LOSING MY APPETITE........................................... 39

NEEDING FINANCIAL ASSISTANCE........................ 44

CAR TROUBLE ..................................................... 47

BATTER UP .......................................................... 51

CHANGING THE LOCKS........................................ 54

MOVING OUT ..................................................... 60

MY ADVICE ......................................................... 65

RESOURCES......................................................... 70

# PREFACE

I know some may wonder why we write about certain things or topics. I feel writing is about having a free spirit. When one writes, one delves into the past, present, or imagines the future. I have found that writing gives me purpose and a sense of accomplishment.

I am not writing this book to bash my husband. I am writing it for women and men who have gone through what I have gone through and for those who are still going through. I didn't know where to go for help. My relationship with GOD is what kept me sane and brought me through it all.

This book is intended to show that with any form of abuse, you must recognize your threshold, stand up for yourself, and NOT allow any abuser of ANY type to manipulate or enslave your consciousness to accept abuse. Why not? According to Genesis 1:26 and Psalms 139:14, YOU were created by GOD, which means you are wonderfully and beautifully made. Nothing should be allowed to mess with that!

Whether this book helps one person or 100 people to get help, then it's worth exposing my personal experiences. It doesn't matter whether it's the verbally abused or the abuser, both can get help through counseling.

## I AM TALKING ABOUT VERBAL ABUSE!

Verbal abuse does not show up on the outside in the form of a bruise or a scar like physical abuse. Verbal abuse is on the inside. It weighs on the heart and in the mind. Most people may not even know when someone is going through or living with the effects of verbal abuse.

# INTRODUCTION

My husband and I met in the late seventies. We liked each other right away. We started dating and we really enjoyed being together. We were so different in many ways, but we both were adventurous. That was one thing we had in common. He was ex-military and I had done some traveling myself. He had friends that lived in other towns and other states. We would go and visit his friends wherever they lived. We had little to no boundaries as to where we would go. We knew very soon that we loved each other, and we vowed that we would be true to each other.

He knew that I had two teenage children. When they met, they really hit it off. He liked them, and they liked him. My family liked him. That made me very happy, and he seemed to be happy too.

After we dated for some months, he told me he had a baby daughter. He wanted me to meet her. He decided to pick her up and bring her to his place so we could meet.

After dating for about a year, he wanted us to take our relationship to the next level. He never really proposed to me, he just said he wanted us to be married. Well, I was okay with that statement because I really loved him. We decided we would have a big church wedding. Since we both had large families, we figured we would have the wedding and reception at my church.

My niece, who was more like a sister, lived in Columbia. She agreed to help me make all the wedding plans. Before we set the date, we had a very serious disagreement and we called off the wedding. We didn't see each other for a while. I was really hurt by what happened.

After a few weeks, he called. We met up and talked. We decided we would put the past behind us and renew our relationship. We both admitted that we loved each other very much and we still wanted to be together.

We started doing things together again, going places, and visiting family and friends. We spent a lot of time with my children, his daughter, and his family.

He was still a part of the military. He was in the reserve, which meant he would serve a weekend each month and he would have to go away for two weeks each year. About 8 or 9 months after we reconciled, he told me he was scheduled to leave in two weeks and he planned to be a married man before his departure. He reminded me that my 38th birthday was coming up soon and he hoped we could get married on that day. Well, I don't have to tell you how HAPPY I WAS. I didn't even think about a wedding or a wedding dress. We went and applied for our marriage license. I told my family and two of my friends who were also my co-workers. One week later, on a Saturday, we went to the Justice of the Peace. Besides the Justice of the Peace, my fiancé, and me, there were only four other people in attendance. My daughter was my maid of honor. My mom and my two co-worker friends also came to show support. They were all so happy for me. Needless to say, that was one of the Happiest Days of my life - August 29, 1981.

# FIRST INCIDENT

Chapter 1

While I was six months pregnant with our daughter, my husband and I were sitting in the living room watching television when he made some innuendoes about foolish things from the past that I would not do.

My daughter was home from college and my son was in his bedroom. My husband started cursing and screaming at me so loud that my son and daughter ran into the living room. "Mom, Pops, what is going on?" they said. "Oh, he is upset about something, but we will be alright," I assured them. He kept screaming at me, so I walked into the kitchen.

He came up behind me, grabbed a handful of my hair, and pulled a handful of hair rollers out. When my daughter saw that, she said, "Mom you have to get out of here." She caught my arm and led me outside. My son decided to stay behind because he had to go to school the next morning. Also, he said he was going to talk to Pops. I guess he felt he could diffuse the situation.

At the time, I didn't have a car. So my daughter and I started walking to my mom's house. Just as we got out of my yard, our neighbor that lived across the road facing us came out in her car. She stopped and told my daughter and me to get in. "I heard all the cursing and screaming at your house. Are you all alright?" she asked. "Yes, my husband is just a little upset," I told her. "Sounds like he is a lot upset," she stated.

About a month later, he was driving me to my doctor's appointment for my checkup. We were about 15 or 20 minutes away when he started to light a cigarette. He took a puff and inhaled it slowly. I looked over at him and saw that it wasn't a regular cigarette. It was what they called a *joint*. I asked him why he was doing that with me in the car when he knew I was pregnant. "Because I want to," he replied. So, I rolled down the window on my side. He asked why I rolled the window down. "Because I am not breathing in that stuff, and I am not going into my doctor's appointment smelling like that stuff," I said. He started cursing and saying that I f***ed up his f***ing high. "You know I don't like you smoking that stuff around me, and I don't want it to affect our baby," I said. "You just want everything your way; you don't know what you're talking about," he told me.

My husband and I were together until July 6, 1986; that was the day I finally left him. Earlier that week, he tried to drive off as I was reaching into the back seat of our car. If I hadn't jumped back as he hit the gas pedal, I guess I would have been killed or seriously injured. About two days after that incident, I tried to talk to him. I thought we had come to an understanding. That was on a Monday morning. He left that evening to go to work. When I saw him again, it was Wednesday afternoon. He had been doing that throughout our marriage. Sometimes, he would leave on Friday or Saturday and I wouldn't see him for a couple of days. When he walked into the house on that day in July, I was getting my last bit of belongings out of the little cottage we were renting. We had lost two homes in less than five years of our marriage.

About two months before that incident, he came home intoxicated one Saturday night. He started accusing me of not wanting to deal with his family or move into his mom's mobile home. At that time, we were living in my cousin's little pool house. I told him I didn't think his family would want us to move into his mom's home. We were both working, so I felt we should be able to afford our own home. My remarks angered him. While he kept cursing at me, he also accused me of thinking I was too good to live in his mom's trailer home.

Our daughter was asleep and I had my youngest son/great nephew with me that weekend. I raised him from the time he was three months old. He never saw my husband act like that before and he told me he wanted to go home to his grandmother's house. I agreed and told him we would leave when my husband went to sleep. I don't know if he heard me or not, but he got our daughter out of her crib and put her in the bed with him. Then, he told me to get the hell on out and that his baby wasn't going anywhere.

My son and I sat down and waited for him to fall asleep. I went into the kitchen to get our baby's formula from the fridge. As I walked back into the living room, I saw my son with our daughter heading for the door. My husband came running out of the bedroom. He grabbed our daughter from my son and struck him. He told him to get his little ass out of his house. I almost lost it, but I wasn't going to do something that I would have ended up in jail for.

I took my son and went outside so I could talk to him and calm him down. When we tried to go back inside, the door was locked. I knocked on the door, called his name, and asked him to open the door. He wouldn't answer or unlock it. I went to a neighbor's house and called the police. The police officer came and we went to the door. The officer identified himself and told him he needed to open the door so he could talk to him. He opened the door just wide enough to talk to the officer and told him he did not need to come into his house. Although the officer tried to get him to open the door and give me our baby, he still refused. In fact, he said if

I wanted to leave, I could just get the hell on.

"Well mam, I can't break in, so I suggest you go someplace for tonight," the officer stated. "No, I am not leaving my baby with him tonight; and he is intoxicated. If I have to sit out here all night, I will," I replied. The officer apologized and left. After the officer left, my husband opened the door, but he wouldn't let me touch or get near our daughter. He slept with her in his arms the entire night.

After that incident, I took our daughter and moved to Columbia, South Carolina with my niece. We only stayed with her about four or five weeks. School was starting back in the fall in my hometown's school district and I needed to be back to go to work. I went back to Wagener, SC and rented an apartment. The apartment was new and very nice.

One Saturday evening, I heard a knock at my front door. When I opened it, there were two men standing there. They said they were my husband's cousins. He told them to go over to his place, and he would be there in a little while. I didn't know why he told them to come because he didn't live there; and I told them just that. I was bit confused, but I did let them come inside to wait for him. "I thought you said you lived here," is what one of the guys said to him once he arrived. "I do sometimes, but this place is so dang small, so I just stay at my house most of the time," he replied. Why is he lying to his cousins like that? Is he trying to make them think we are together? Those were the questions in my head.

Our daughter, my son, and I lived in the apartment about eighteen months. Then we moved back to Columbia. I worked temporary jobs until I got a full-time job in the school district. When our daughter turned three, I enrolled her in preschool. During our entire time there, I got very little help from my husband. Although I filed for child support, I only received about eight checks the entire time.

For years, he didn't try to contact our daughter or me. I heard he was living with a woman who had two girls. When she was six years old, he came to take our daughter shopping for a coat. I didn't realize that he brought the woman with him, until he brought our daughter back home and I noticed she was in the car as he was backing out of the driveway.

About two years later, we went to see my son and his family. My husband was actually there with his daughter that he had before we married and her child. When we came in, he spoke and left. That was the last time our daughter saw him until after she graduated high school and had gone to college. She wanted her father in her life. She even reached out to some of his family members to ask him to come to her graduation.

In 1996, my niece retired from her state job. She was diagnosed with Multiple Sclerosis. My daughter and I took care of her and shared a bedroom. In 1997, my niece had a new handicapped accessible home built, and she wanted my daughter to have her own room.

Ten years later, my husband contacted me and asked how our daughter was doing. He heard that she lost a friend in college and that she wasn't taking it very well. I told him she was in Virginia with her sister and her family and that I would tell her he called. When she graduated from a Massage Therapy School in Virginia, I drove and picked her up. When we got back to Columbia, she called her dad and asked him if he would come to Columbia and go out to dinner with her. He did come and she took him out to dinner. After that, we stayed in contact with each other off and on.

I eventually retired from the school district in 2006. At that time, my niece's health declined to the point that she couldn't be left at home alone, not even for a few hours. We traveled a lot after my retirement. We went to Virginia several times a year. We took my husband there a few times to help our daughter and son-in-law with a home they were building. Sadly, four years later, in March 2010, my niece passed. She willed the house and everything she owned to me.

# RECONNECTING

Chapter 2

On New Year's Eve in 2010, our daughter and I moved to Charlotte, North Carolina. Things went well for a while. We both got jobs in retail. That was not what either of us were looking for, but that was the only field we could get employment in at that time. We worked on opposite sides of the city, but we made it work with my one car.

We found a wonderful church and church family. They took us into their church and their family as if they had known us forever. In April, during our Church Conference, my two sons and their wives came up on Sunday and brought my husband with them. By then, he was no longer living with the other woman and had reconnected with the family.

My daughter in Virginia found him a car and she and her three sons were meeting him in Petersburg, Virginia, to get it. After church, our daughter and I took him to Petersburg to meet them and get his car. Earlier, she asked me if he could move into my house in Columbia since I was not living there now. I thought about it and agreed. The rent he would pay would help with the mortgage. He told her he gotten some type of financial settlement, but he never mentioned it to me. I didn't find out about it until we got back to Charlotte a little after 1:00 a.m. on Monday morning. He stayed at our apartment. I gave him my bed; and I slept on the couch.

A few hours later, we woke up. Before he left, our daughter asked him if he could help her out financially. He took her to the bank and gave her $150. While he was on the road, he called me and told me he couldn't afford to take care of two homes or give her money because he had to pay his own rent and his own bills.

In May 2011, I started having car trouble. The mechanic I was referred to seemed to do more harm than good to my car. I borrowed money to get it fixed because that was the only transportation we had. We were living in a fairly new area so there were no bus lines close to us. In June, the transmission went out in my car. I had to quit work because I was working in another town south of Charlotte. I took my car back to the same mechanic and it just sat there. He said he had to order a transmission and I would have to pay him to have it shipped to his shop. By the end of June, it still wasn't repaired. I had no choice but to move back home.

I called my husband and asked him if he would mind if we moved back home. I could have said, "You need to move out, so we can move back in our house." But, I tried to be nice. I also knew his living conditions before he moved into my home wasn't the best. He said he had been praying and asking God to help him get his family back and he claimed he was so happy it was happening.

# CHILD SUPPORT

Chapter 3

I rented a moving truck on July 6, 2011. He got some guys he knew from the area to help him move me back home. Our daughter didn't want to come back, so she stayed another week trying to get to her two jobs. It didn't work out, so she called some friends from Columbia to help her move back home. She found a job in a week or two after she moved back. It was hard for me to find work since most of my experience was working in the school district or childcare. Because of that, my husband told me not to worry about working right now and that he would take care of me.

A month or so after I moved back, my husband asked me to drop the child support case. I don't know if the Department of Social Services (DSS) had contacted him or not. By then, he owed me over $35,000 in back child support. He told me he couldn't pay the mortgage if he had to pay child support. My daughter in Virginia stopped helping with the mortgage after I moved back. I told him I tried to drop it years ago, but the judge said I couldn't until she was an adult. He said that wasn't true because some of his friends' baby mothers had dropped theirs. Since I wasn't working and our daughter was an adult now, I agreed to drop the case because he never helped me take care of her anyway. The social worker told me that if I dropped the case, I could never open it again. I told him it was okay.

# THE ABUSE BEGINS

Chapter 4

One Saturday afternoon in early September 2011, the three of us went to my grandson's college to see him play football. We had a wonderful time at the game with my son, his wife, and her family. The men were having their drinks, and the women were cheering the game on. After leaving the stadium after the game, our daughter was driving us back home. We were in my husband's car. He told our daughter she needed to change her plans for tomorrow so she could be home to meet one of his nephews who was coming by. "No dad," she said, "I don't want to change my plans to meet someone who has never tried to contact me before." She continued to say, "I am an adult now and he has never tried to see me before."

He got angry, started cursing and screaming at our daughter, and using the f-word. She started screaming, crying, and shaking. I told her to pull over. After she stopped the car, I told her we were getting out. We got out and walked back to the stadium. It took us about 10 minutes, but we got there just in time to catch my son before he left.

My car was still broken at the time, so we had been using his car to get our daughter to and from work. Well, needless to say, she and I walked downtown to the bus transit station and she bought tokens to ride the bus to and from work. The following week, I had a talk with our daughter and a one-on-one talk with him. They both agreed to apologize to each other. I told them how proud I was of them. Things got back to normal for a while.

When my sister-in-law passed, my car was still not working. She lived in the town of Wagener, SC. My husband and I left Columbia early so we could head to Wagener and spend some time with the family before going to the church for the funeral. We were at my nephew's home for about 30 minutes when he told me he needed to leave. He said he was going to one of his nephew's house to borrow some money. Because we were going to be leaving soon to go the funeral, I asked him if we could go to his nephew's home after the funeral service was over. "No, I need to go now while he is at home. I will be back before then," he said as he left. When the family car came to pick up the children and their families, he still had not come back. As everyone else got into his or her cars to go to the church, I stood in the yard wondering how in the world I was going to get to the church. No one even offered me a ride. Just as everyone was leaving, my nephew from Columbia drove up, parked on the side of the road, and waited for all the other cars to pull out. I called to him. He got out of his truck, came over to me, and asked me why I was standing out there in the yard alone. After I told him why, he could not believe my husband left me there and had not come back. He told me I could ride to church with him, but he wasn't going to stay for the entire service. He had to get back to Columbia and go to work.

We went to the church, my nephew spoke to a few people, and then he said he was leaving. I wanted to stay for the funeral. I felt that my husband would come before it was over. I sat through most of the service. I never did see him inside the church, so I went outside to look for him. I didn't see him or his car. As I stood outside, a couple of people I went to high school with started talking to me. I was a bit distracted because I was talking and looking for him at the same time. He never showed up.

After a while, a family member, who was also a friend of mine, came outside and we started talking. She also lived in Columbia. I told her what happened and I asked her if I could get a ride back with her. I offered to pay her as well. "Of course, you can ride back with me, but you can't pay me anything," she said. WOW, I was so grateful to GOD and her. I was also angry and hurt. He came home sometime that night. I asked him why he left me and never showed up again, knowing that I didn't have a ride. He said he was at the cemetery waiting for me. "Well, how was I supposed to get to the cemetery?" I asked. "Well, I thought you would catch a ride with some of the family," he said.

One Sunday afternoon, one of his cousins was speaking at a church in an area outside of Columbia. He wanted our daughter and me to go with him. We got dressed and got in the car with him to go to the church. Instead of going directly to the church, we stopped at his aunt's house in Columbia. We thought he was probably picking her up to ride with us. He told us to get out and go inside. "No, we will wait here in the car," we both replied. We were still thinking he was going inside to get her and we would be leaving. Our daughter and I sat in the car for about 45 minutes or so. No one came out. After about 10 more minutes, our daughter called a friend of hers to come pick her up and take her back home. She asked me if I wanted to go back home too. I said, "No, I'll wait for your dad." After she left, I sat in the car and shortly afterwards, another car drove up and parked. Some people got out and went inside. As soon as they went inside, people started coming out getting into two cars.

My husband came out and got into the car. When he didn't see our daughter, he asked where she was. I told him she got tired of waiting so she went back home. He asked how she went, and I said she called a friend to pick her up. He started the car and began cursing at me and calling me names. He told me that I was a very bad person. He said that I caused him problems and I was the reason our daughter didn't respect him. All the way to the church, he went on about what a bad and selfish person I was. I asked him why he was so angry with me and what had I done to make him so angry. He said, "You are so damn selfish." "If I was so selfish, I wouldn't have sat out there in the car and waited for you when you didn't even have the courtesy to tell me you were waiting for other people to come," I replied. When we got to the church, of course, he acted like the perfect gentleman. He introduced me to some of his family members I didn't know.

# APPOINTMENTS

Chapter 5

In early spring 2012, my oldest daughter and my youngest son bought a transmission for my car. One of my nephews and my husband went to Charlotte and towed it to Columbia in the fall of 2011. I called my mechanic in Lexington, who is also a good friend of the family, to come and tow my car to his shop to fix it. All this time, my husband hadn't offered me a penny to help get my car fixed. It had been sitting in our yard for about six months. I paid the mechanic for fixing it.

About a week later, he said he wanted to go to Beaufort, SC to talk to some people about starting a seafood business. Of course, he wanted to drive my car, so my oldest son went with us to Beaufort. Shortly after that, he said something was wrong with his car. So, I started taking him to his appointments in Aiken and Augusta, Georgia every week, sometimes twice a week. One day, as we left his doctor's office in Aiken, we went to Sam's Club to gas up. On the way there, he asked me a question and when I answered, he didn't like the answer. He started calling me stupid ass and ignorant ass. He cursed and called me names all the way to the gas station.

When we got there, he got out to pump the gas. He was cursing and calling me names so loud that it got the attention of a lady at a tank across from us. She looked at him. I could tell she was nervous. She stopped pumping and looked at him and then at me. She hurried and got into her car and drove off. A man right next to us drawing gas looked at my husband and then looked at me and shook his head. I was so hurt and embarrassed. When he got back in the car, he kept on cursing and name-calling. I just drove and tried to ignore him.

A few weeks later, he went over to the Veterans Medical Center in Columbia. He called me about 12:30 to come pick him up. When I got there, he told me he had to go to Aiken for an appointment. On our way there, he was talking on his phone with someone. As I got on I-77, which turns into I-26, he said he was going to show me a shortcut. He was too busy still talking on the phone, when I passed the exit he was talking about, which wouldn't have been shorter anyway, in my opinion. When he looked up and saw that I passed the exit, he put his phone down and asked me why I hadn't taken the exit. "I didn't know which one you were talking about, but I know how to go the way we usually go," I responded. He began saying, "You are so damn stupid. No one can tell your stupid ass a f***ing thing. I know what I'm talking about. That's why I told your damn ignorant ass to go that way." I just kept driving. I was so angry. I told myself that if I saw a policeman anywhere I would stop and ask him to make him get out of my car. I didn't see one, so I took him on to Aiken.

Another time after that, I took him to Aiken for an appointment. That day he had two, one before noon and one later afternoon. In between the appointment times, he asked me if I wanted to go and get something to drink. "Yes, that would be nice," I replied. We went to a McDonald's. I parked the car and he went in to get our drinks. When he got out, he told me I parked crooked. I said, "Well, you will be back out in a few minutes and there are lots of spaces between the other cars and my car." When he came out with our drinks and got in the car, he told me I was so selfish because I took up two parking spaces. "I wasn't that far in the other space and I would have moved if I needed to. Plus, no one parked near me anyway," I said. He said, "I just can't believe you could be so damn selfish. You only think about yourself." He kept saying things like that all the way back to the doctor's office. I told him it's not worth us arguing about.

When we got back to the doctor's office, he jumped out the car and slammed the door. He just left me sitting there in the car. I got out, went in, and sat next to him.

Of course, he ignored me. When the doctor called him, he just got up, didn't look at me, and went on back.

In November 2012, my nephew, a Public Safety Officer, who lives in Aiken, invited me to a dinner/gala. They always have it each year for the senior citizens. He told me a lady I used to work with in Aiken years ago always asked him about me after she found out he was my nephew. She was also on the planning committee for the Gala. He didn't tell her he asked me to come as his guest, because he wanted to surprise her. I told him I would love to attend. My husband said he would love to go when I invited him.

We left Columbia early on the day of the Gala, so I could stop in Lexington and submit an application for a job my son told me about. When we got there, he told me to get out at the door entrance and he would park the car. "Okay, good, thanks," I said. When I finished the application and came out, he started driving. When I noticed the radio wasn't on the gospel station, I just automatically turned it back to that station. He said, "What are you doing?" I replied, "Oh, I just put it back on the station." He said, "It was on a station so why did you change it?" I said, "You know we always listen to the gospel station." He said, "I was listening to it." "You know I don't listen to that kind of music," I said. "There you go with your old selfish ass," he said. "When I am in your car, I respect your rights and I don't touch anything. So, please respect mine in my car," I told him.

I really don't listen to that kind of music with all the cursing and talking bad about women.

He started with the name-calling and put-downs. "Why does every damn thing have to be like you want it? Who the hell do you think you are anyway?" he asked. He went on and on calling me old ass, stupid ass, and selfish ass. By the time we got on I-20, I was so hurt and angry. I told him to turn around and go back home. By then, I was in no mood to go to the Gala. He turned the car around and we started back home. I asked him why he had such evil thoughts about me when all I have tried to do was be there for him. "Because your old ass is evil," he said. "If I'm so evil, then maybe you need to get from around me," I told him.

# THREE DAYS & TWO NIGHTS

Chapter 6

I applied for work in November 2012, but I didn't receive a call from the company until late January 2013 notifying me that they were interested. I attended orientation on February 4th, and I started working the following week. On the first week in March, my husband left home on a Tuesday morning. He said he was taking some family reunion letters to some family members in Wagener. On Wednesday evening, I started to worry, so I called his two brothers to see if he had gotten in touch with them and I wanted them to know what he was doing. One of his brothers did hear from him because he came to practice for his quartet-singing group. I didn't see or hear from him again until Thursday evening when I got home from work. He was lying on the chaise watching television. When I walked in, he didn't say anything. He just laid there with his feet up on the chaise as if he hadn't been away at all. He offered no explanation at all. He didn't even speak to me.

After about an hour, I asked him where he had been for three days and two nights. He said he had been in the Veterans Hospital in Augusta, GA. I knew he was lying so I asked him why he didn't call me. He didn't say anything, so I asked him if I could see his release papers. He told me they were in the car. When I got home from work on the next day, I asked him again to show me the release papers. "Since you are calling me a liar, I am not going to show you nothing," he said. "I know you're not because they don't exist," I said. "There you go starting some damn shit again. You think you know every damn thing," he said. After that, I didn't say anything else to him.

When I left for work the next morning, I told him he could leave because I was tired of him with his lies and disrespect. He laughed and mumbled something under his breath. When I came home from work that evening, he was lying on the chaise lounge. That angered me, so I called the police and told them I had a domestic problem I needed help with. When they came, he was l lying on the bed. They asked me if he had struck me. "No, I just want him out of my house and out of my life," I stated. They went in and talked to him. He told them he hadn't done anything, and he didn't know why they came. Once they told him why they came, he just replied, "Oh." They asked me to walk back outside with them. They informed me that they couldn't do anything if he hadn't physically abused me. So one of us must hurt the other to get any help. That's the thought that flashed in my mind.

I didn't talk to him for a while, but I still cooked for him and went to church with him. I wasn't a person who could hold anger in me. I just couldn't stay mad long. He never accepted any wrongdoing or gave any apologies. I was always the one to forgive and try to make the marriage work. Even when we weren't getting along, I still made sure he got to his appointments.

No matter how much I tried to help him, he still continued to not come home when he should. I remember one Saturday afternoon he told me that he was going to visit some of his cousins in another town about 25 or 30 miles from Columbia. I went to work at 4:00 p.m. When I got home about 12:30 a.m., he wasn't there. I got a call from him about 1:30 a.m. saying he was going to Augusta with his cousins. When I saw him again it was Sunday night. He said that his cousins wanted him to spend time with them, so that's why he didn't come home. I didn't even say anything back to him.

# SURGERY

## Chapter 7

In June 2013, my husband and I were not getting along at the time, so I took my son with me to help me look for a car. I came home with a brand-new car. After three or four days of driving the car, he asked me what I was going to do about it. "What do you mean? What am I going to do about it? I bought it," I said. "Oh, you bought it, well you didn't tell me anything," he replied.

Soon after that, his car went out again. When he had appointments during my work hours, which were all three shifts, I let him drive my car. If I worked 12:00 midnight to 8:00 a.m., I would go home, take a shower, and then take him to Aiken or Augusta, wherever his appointment was.

We got along good for a few months. Then, he started hanging out with a guy friend of his who was divorced. I didn't really know the guy. I heard his name a few times when I was living near Wagener. I didn't even know he lived in Columbia. I never really met him.

At least once every other week, my husband would spend the night with him. If he wasn't driving, the guy would pick him up, and he would tell me he was going to the guy's apartment. I wouldn't see him again until the next day. I told him I didn't like him staying out and hanging out all the time with a single man. He told me that was his friend and he would visit and hang out with him any damn time he wanted to. "Well, why don't you just move over there with him, since you don't have any respect for me when it comes to him," I said. "You are full of damn shit with your old stupid ass," he responded. The every-other-week-sleepover went on for months. I didn't say anything else to him about it. However, I still went to church with him every Sunday. I went to church programs with him at his church. I very seldom went to my church and he never went with me when I did.

In July 2013, our daughter quit her job in Columbia and moved to the Atlanta, Georgia area. She had enough. She couldn't stay in the same house with her dad any longer and see how disrespectfully he talked to me.

In April 2014, I planned a surprise birthday party for our daughter and my husband since their birthdays were only about a month apart. Two of Tamara's (our youngest daughter) friends and my two sons helped me plan and get everything together.

My oldest son and my nephew took my husband to a

church outing for men that Saturday morning, while my youngest son and I got everything set up in the backyard. Our daughter had already planned to come to Columbia that Saturday to get her hair done by a friend of hers. When I spoke to her friend, I told her to keep my daughter occupied until I call and let her know when it was time to come to the house.

Our daughter got there a short time before we finished setting up. She was so surprised and happy. After everyone I invited arrived, I called my son and told him that everything was ready and he could bring my husband on. When they arrived, he saw all the people and how beautifully we had the backyard decorated. I could tell he was surprised.

We had a wonderful time. Everyone had fun and said what a good job I did with all the food and decorations. I thanked everyone for helping me and for coming to celebrate with our daughter and him.

After everyone left and our daughter had gone out with some of her friends, my husband and I sat in the living room. I asked him if he enjoyed his surprise. He said, "Oh, that wasn't no surprise. I knew what you were doing all the time." I knew he didn't know, but, of course, he couldn't allow me to take credit for doing anything good. I made up my mind right then that I would never, ever, spend my time, energy, and money trying to do anything extra for him again.

On one afternoon, during the first week in April

2015, he left in his truck to get some crossties from somewhere beside a railroad track. He told me they had been discarded by the railroad workers and if anyone wanted them all they had to do was come and get them. His truck got stuck and he couldn't get it out. He called my son and told him where the truck was. When my son and his son got off from work, they went to help him get the truck. They couldn't get it, so they brought him home about 9:30 that night.

I was lying down on the couch watching television when they brought him home. He took a shower and came back into the living room. He asked me something about a cake my daughter bought me. I didn't hear exactly what he asked me so I said, "Say what?" Wow! You would have thought I committed a crime. He started cursing in a very loud voice and then he went into the bedroom. A minute later, he came back in the living room and called me a name. That was such a shock to me. I wasn't sure I heard him right. "What did you just say?" I asked. "You heard me. I said bitch. You stupid old ass, old ignorant ass bitch," he said bluntly. I was in total shock. He had never gone that far with his verbal insults. I couldn't say anything. I couldn't even cry. I was just in shock and disbelief. He kept repeating it for several minutes. He laid down on the chaise and just kept cursing at me and calling me names. Finally, I heard him snoring, so I went upstairs to bed. I don't remember if I slept that night or not.

A couple of weeks later, his doctor in Augusta told him he needed to have shoulder surgery. The doctor scheduled his surgery for June 1st. Of course, I had to take him. We got to the hospital at 6:20 a.m. on Monday morning. I sat by his bed in a small, hard chair. There was no soft chair in sight. We were there four days and three nights. Guess what? This bitch was the only person there. No one came to see him the entire time. When I started putting our things in the car on Thursday evening, it was the first time I had been out to my car since we went inside the hospital.

He had been home for little over a week before the basketball playoffs. That Tuesday, the day of the playoffs, I went to the store and got stuff to make snacks for us to have during the game. I thought that we would watch it together since he was still recuperating.

As I fixed the food for us, I noticed he was outside on his phone. He usually sat on the porch to smoke and drink, so I didn't think too much about it. Just as I finished and put the food on the coffee table, he came to the front door, stuck his head in, and told me he was going to his friend's house to watch the game. That was hurtful. He knew I was expecting us to watch it together. I looked outside and saw him getting into his friend's truck. When I saw him again, it was the next morning. He and his friend walked in and he handed me a McDonald's bag like I was some kind of puppy. "No thanks," I said. He went in the bedroom, came back out, and they left again. He said they were going over to the Veterans Medical Center. Again, he provided no explanation or reason why he left and stayed out all night.

# FORECLOSURE

Chapter 8

One day, while I was outside working in the yard, I picked up a lot of old junk and stuff laying around. He came out and saw me putting junk by the curb for the trash pickup. He said, "What the hell are you doing?" I said, "I am cleaning up the yard and getting rid of some of this stuff that's just laying here making it look so junky around here." Before my niece passed, we had one of the most beautiful yards on the block. He saw the junk I had already put out and said, "That is my damn stuff and I didn't tell you to touch it." "This stuff has been cluttering up the yard for months and it's not useable," I pointed out to him.

"That is my stuff and you keep your damn stupid hands off it!" he exclaimed. He went to the curb and started bringing the junk back in the yard.

My oldest grandson in Virginia was getting married on Saturday, July 11, 2015. Our daughter and I drove up on Wednesday evening after she got to Columbia from Marietta, GA. We drove my car and left her car for her dad and her brother to drive on Thursday night. Her brother had to work all day Thursday and her dad said he had an appointment Thursday morning. We got there about 2:00 a.m. Thursday morning. Our daughter was going to sing at the wedding. Her dad and brother got there about 4:30 a.m. Friday morning. About 9:30 that Friday morning, the guys went outside to the pool. About an hour later, one of the guys came in and asked me to call the paramedics. He said my husband jumped into the pool and passed out. They had to get him out of the pool and they were trying to revive him. I picked up my phone and ran outside to where he was. By then, he was breathing on his own, so my son-in-law said I didn't have to call the paramedics. I went back inside for a minute or two. When I returned outside, I saw that he was having trouble breathing again, so I immediately called the paramedics. We took him to the hospital. The doctor told me he could have died, if we hadn't brought him in because he had water in his lungs. My son, our daughter, and I sat with him for a few hours until our daughter had to leave to go to the church to rehearse for her songs.

On Saturday morning before the wedding, we went back to the hospital and sat with him until it was time to get dressed. Needless to say, he missed the wedding. Our daughter and I went back to the hospital on Sunday. He was supposed to be dismissed, but the doctor wasn't there when we got there. We stayed a while, then we went back to get my daughter house to pack. I called and asked him if the doctor came back and if he was going to be dismissed. He said he didn't know yet. I said, "Well, I may have to go home because I have an appointment tomorrow and our daughter has to go back to Marietta. I will come back on Monday after I leave my appointment to get you. If you are dismissed before I get back Monday, my daughter said she would come to pick you up." He hung up the phone on me. He was dismissed later that Sunday afternoon. As promised, our daughter and I went to pick him up. We left Virginia late Sunday afternoon on July 12th.

On July 14th, my daughter called me from Virginia to ask me if I knew my husband was moving out. I told her he didn't say anything to me about moving. She mentioned when he was up there for the wedding that he was moving in with a friend. I wish he had told me earlier, so I could have gone back to work. "So that's why he hasn't given me the mortgage money for the past two months. He was planning on letting me lose my home and he was going to live someplace else," I said.

Since I hadn't worked since January, I had no money to pay the mortgage and he knew that.

A week passed and he still hadn't said anything to me about leaving, so I asked him about it. "Yes, I'm moving. You're always telling me to leave, so I'm leaving," he said. "Well, I wish you would have told me. I would have gone back to work, even if the doctor didn't approve," I told him.

August came and he was still there, but he wasn't paying any bills. I was paying the electric and the water bill, but I didn't have enough to pay the mortgage. On August 9th, he started with the names again. He cursed and called me old ass, ignorant ass, and dumb ass. I just stopped communicating with him altogether. I stopped cooking for him too. The next day, he started again calling me a dumb ass and a selfish ass. I told him he needed to get his things and leave since we were losing the house anyway. He didn't have any furniture. All he had were his clothes and some junk outside. When he went outside to sit on the porch, I went inside and sat on the couch. When he came inside, he walked by me, looked at me with a smirk on his face, shook his head and said, "Stupid ass self." "I thought you were leaving?" I said. "Your old evil ass can't make me go nowhere and if you call the cops, they are just going to say, another stupid black woman," he said.

On August 12th, I'd had enough. I started packing my clothes, dishes, and utensils. I called the Salvation

Army to come pick up the furniture from the two upstairs bedrooms. I called my son and told him I needed someone with a truck to move my washer and dryer to Marietta, GA to his sister's house, because I couldn't take the verbal abuse and disrespect anymore. I told him I wasn't going to jail for him because he wasn't worth it. So, the best thing for me to do was leave, since he wouldn't.

On August 15th, the mortgage was three months past due. UPS left a notice on my front door about foreclosure. I went out on the porch where he was sitting, smoking, and drinking. I told him he needed to leave today and I was not playing. I went back inside and started putting my boxes together.

About 20 minutes later, I heard a knock on the door. The door opened and two cops walked in. One of them told me my husband had called them because I was trying to make him leave the house. I told him we were losing the house to the mortgage company and if I have to move, then he needs to move too. "Well, it looks like you are already packed. So why don't you just go ahead and leave and let the bank evict him," the officer said while looking at all the boxes. All the while, he was standing behind the two officers looking at me with a smirk on his face. When they left, he went back on the porch. I was so hurt. I couldn't believe he had stooped so low since he was the one saying he was moving ever since July. WOW!!! I was flabbergasted. I called my son at work and asked him to come as soon as he could get there after he and his son got off work. I wanted him to come and get my stuff so I could leave. We got to Marietta at 2:15 a.m. Because they both had to work that day, they left Marietta around 3:30 a.m. on the way to Columbia.

# LOSING MY APPETITE

Chapter 9

I lived with our daughter in Marietta until September 7th, which was Labor Day. I hadn't been able to find any kind of employment. I tried at different businesses, but no one hired me. Since I hadn't been able to find employment in Marietta and he was still living in my home in Columbia, I called him and told him I was coming back on Labor Day. He said it was okay but to be careful on the road because the State Troopers were out there. I told him I will. Evidently, my husband, my daughter in Virginia, and her husband had caught the mortgage up when they had come down in August after I left.

I left Marietta 8:00 a.m. on Labor Day. I got to Columbia around noon. In the meantime, I called some places in Columbia about employment. I kept in touch with one of my former supervisors. She said they had openings and since I was a good and dependable employee, she was sure the company would hire me again.

When I arrived home, he was outside on the driveway. He asked if I needed him to take anything inside for me. I told him I didn't because I only had my clothes. I took my things upstairs and unpacked. The next morning, he said he had an appointment in Augusta and he didn't know if his car would make it there and back. He bought an old Plymouth Volare from one of his nephews. When he said that about his car, I knew what he was doing so I immediately asked him if he wanted me to take him. "Yes, that would be better than me taking a chance on my car," he said. I took him to Augusta. When we got back to Columbia, I took him to three different auto parts stores to look for what he needed for his car.

Things went well the rest of that week. I went to church with him that Sunday morning. Everything also went well the second week, until Friday night. We watched television Friday night. He had been drinking earlier. He got a call. When he finished talking, he asked me to take him to Wal-Mart. We went to one that wasn't too far from us. We laughed, joked, and enjoyed each other's company. When we left the store, he asked me if I wanted to stop at Wendy's to get something to eat. I told him that was fine with me. I pulled in and we went inside to order our food. While we were waiting, I walked to the soda dispenser to get my drink. When I came back to the end of the counter where I had left him, I didn't see him. My food was on the counter, so I picked it up and stood there a few minutes. When I still didn't see him, I went to the car. Since I didn't notice any other food on the counter, I figured he may have gotten his food and went to the car. When I got to the car, he wasn't there, so I just got in and waited. Then, I figured he must be in the restroom.

I was in the car a minute or two before he came out. He came to the car, jerked the door open, and started cursing. "Why the hell did you walk out and leave my damn food on the counter?" He asked in an abrasive manner. I was in total shock! I said, "What? What are you talking about?" He said, "You know what the hell I'm talking about, you left my f***ing food on the damn counter." "I did not leave your food, it wasn't on the counter when I came out and I didn't know if you had got it and came out or not," I said. "You are just so damn selfish. You don't think about nobody but your damn self," he said. "I told you your food was not on the counter," I said. He kept cursing as I drove home. "Is it worth all of this? Why are you so angry?" I asked. He said, "You're f***ing evil, selfish old ass." He cursed and called me names all the way home. When I parked and we got out, he was cursing so loud I saw some of the neighbor's lights come on.

I couldn't eat that night. I got very little sleep, and I didn't go to bed at all. I tried to sleep on the couch, but

I was so upset I started having severe pain in my stomach. I told myself I couldn't take this anymore. About 5:30 a.m., I got up and started putting my clothes back in my car. He was on the chaise on the other side. When he woke up and saw me putting my clothes in my car, he asked me what I was doing. I told him I was putting my things in the car. He asked me, "Why?" "I'm leaving," I said. "Where are you going?" he asked. I told him, "I'm going back to Georgia." He said okay and mumbled something else that I couldn't understand.

By 6:00 a.m., I was heading out. I didn't know if I would make it back to Marietta or not, the pain was so bad, but I knew I couldn't stay there anymore. After I got on the road, I called our daughter and told her I was heading back. I didn't tell her how sick I was until I was almost there. My daughter from Virginia was at Myrtle Beach, SC with her in-laws. I called her and told her what happened. We talked for a while. I told her I hadn't told her sister I was in pain because she had to work that day and I knew she would have taken off and tried to come get me. My oldest daughter told me to call the paramedics when I got to Marietta and have them take me to the emergency room.

When I got to our daughter's apartment, she had already gone to her weekend job at the furniture store. I was in so much pain. I tried not to call the paramedics, but after about an hour after I got there, the pain didn't lessen any. I finally decided to call them and they came and took me to the emergency room. Our daughter came a little later and stayed with me until I was released from the hospital. Next week he called me and asked why I didn't let him know I was in the hospital. I almost laughed.

By the end of the year, I still hadn't found a job. Our daughter knew I was feeling really bad about her having to take care of me financially, so she planned a surprise Christmas trip for me. She took me to North Carolina to our Bishop and Lady Bishop's home. We had a wonderful time. When we got back to Georgia, she had another surprise for me. My children had gotten together and bought me a ticket for the Panther's game in Atlanta. Wow! It was an awesome Christmas.

# NEEDING FINANCIAL ASSISTANCE

Chapter 10

On January 2, 2016, I texted him and asked him if he would put $100 in my bank account. I didn't hear from him for two days, so I texted him again on January 5th and asked if he was going to do it or not. He called and said his car was in the shop and he had to use his money to get it out. He said he didn't know if he could borrow any money or not. A few days later, he texted me and asked for my account number. When he did that, I thought he was going to deposit the money. I didn't hear from him again and the money was never deposited. On January 9th, he called our daughter at work. He told her that I asked him for a favor, but he wasn't able to do it.

One evening in January, our daughter and I were getting ready to go to the laundromat. I got a call from him. He started talking about something he read in the

Bible. "In the Bible," he said, "it says that everyone should take responsibility for their own actions. I also read where it said both people have to work together to make a marriage work." I told him, "That's exactly how it should be, and that's what I've been trying to do. But I can't make a marriage work by myself. You are always cursing at me and calling me names for no reason. I never called you names. When I did react to your verbal abuse and said something I shouldn't have, I apologized immediately." He kept on talking and trying to convince me that everything was my fault. I told him I was busy getting ready to go to the laundromat, so he could call me later if he wanted to.

What he didn't know was that every time he called me names and cursed me, I would get my Bible and read or pray. That's how I dealt with those situations. Otherwise, I think I would have lost it and maybe did something I would have regretted later.

A few days later, he called me about 11:00 a.m. "I thought you were going to call me back," he said. I reminded him that I told him if he wanted to, he could call me back later because I was going to the laundromat. He said, "Well, I apologize for what I said the other day, or what you think I said." "So, you can't or won't admit to yourself or me that you called me names and cursed me?" I asked. "Well, like I said, if that's what you think I said," he said. "Well, you know how you feel, and I know how I feel. Since we can't agree on anything, there is no reason for us to continue this conversation," I said. We didn't talk for a while after that.

In February 2016, on Super Bowl Sunday, we went to my youngest son's family's home in Lexington to watch the game. My husband was there also. That was the first time I saw him in months. We spoke and that was it.

# CAR TROUBLE

Chapter 11

During the first week in April 2016, our daughter completed an application for me online for a position as a Health-Caregiver/Companion. We thought it was for a position in Georgia. The next day, I got a call asking me to come to Lexington, SC in two days for an interview. I packed and went home to Columbia. I called him first and told him I was coming. He told me he would see me when I got there.

When I got there, we brought my things inside. We talked for a while. He told me his brother was in a nursing home facility in Columbia, and his cousin was in the hospital with cancer. I asked him if he would like to go see them. He said he would like to see them tomorrow.

The next morning, which was Wednesday, when we got ready to go visit his brother and cousin, I asked him if he was planning to drive his car, or if he wanted me to drive my car. He said his car wasn't running so well, so

I had to drive. We visited his brother first, and then we went to the hospital to visit his cousin.

On Thursday, I went for my interview, which turned out to be an in-service training session for about seven of us. We were already hired. I was so happy. I had two more days of training the next week before I started work. He rode with me to the interview. When I went inside, I forgot to manually turn the headlights off. When we came out, my car would not start. There was a man who parked a few spaces up from us. I walked over to him and asked if he would give us a boost. "Yes, sure I will," he said. He asked my husband to help him roll my car away from the curb a little. My husband tried to put my car in gear to roll it backwards. Unfortunately, it would not change gears unless the engine was on. The man figured out a way to get to the battery and he got it started. Later that day, when we got back to Columbia, my husband said he needed to go by his mechanic's shop to ask him about a part he needed for his car.

When we got there, he got out, and the mechanic walked over to the car and spoke. He asked a question about my car and before I could answer him, my husband said, "That damn thing won't even change gears if it's not started." He also made another put-down comment about my car. The young man looked at him and said, "It's better than that thing you drive. I'm tired of trying to fix that thing every other week. Maybe you need to get you a car like hers."

I had been home almost two weeks. We sat in the living room watching television that Saturday morning. He got a call. When he finished talking, he told me it was a friend. Then, he told me who the friend was. He met a guy when we were separated and he was living with the other woman. I had met the guy before.

He waited a few minutes and then he told me he needed to go to the truck stop and pick him up because he just got there and parked his rig. "Oh, he wants to come here a while before he gets back on the road" I said. He said, "No, he is coming here to stay. I told him he could move in with me this weekend." I was floored. WOW!! "What did you say?" I asked. "That's my friend and I told him he could move in here with me." "No, he is not moving in here," I said assertively. "Why?" he asked. I said, "Because I'm living here now, he cannot stay here." He said, "That doesn't make any difference." I said, "Yes, it does, and he is not moving in here." "I am the man of this house and I can move anyone I want to in here," he stated. "No, you can't and if he comes up in here, I will have the police bar him from the property," I said. "Well, you can get the hell out of here!" he exclaimed. I said, "I am back to stay, and I am not going anywhere. So, if you want to live with your friend, then the two of you need to get a place together but it won't be here!" He ranted, cursed, and called me names. I didn't say anything else to him.

About two weeks later, I contacted my previous job

and was told to come do another application. I did the application and was told that I could start orientation the next week. As soon as I finished a week of orientation, I started on my second job. We weren't talking to each other, but I still cooked for him.

About two weeks after that, he left home one Sunday after church and I didn't see or hear from him until he came back Thursday evening. He didn't say where he had been, and I didn't ask him. The next week, he left on Monday and when he came back, it was Friday. He still didn't say where he was. That went on for a month before I found out where he was staying. I was talking to a family member and they told me his cousin had been moved to the cancer center in Newnan, GA. He was going there and staying with him. After a couple of months, his cousin was brought back to Columbia. I would take him to visit him and we would spend time with him as often as we could.

# BATTER UP

Chapter 12

The day started out beautifully on Labor Day, September 5, 2016. He asked me if I wanted to ride to Augusta with him. He had gotten his car out of the shop. I asked him if he had a doctor's appointment. He said he didn't, but he wanted to go to the Augusta Mall. I replied and said, "Yes, I would love to go to the mall. I need to buy some shoes anyway." When we started out, he said he had to take his phone there to get it repaired. My daughter in Virginia had gotten him a phone on her plan. We were in GA most of the day. We had lunch in the mall's food court, while we waited for his phone.

When we got back home, I turned on the television to watch the news. The announcer said the Columbia Fireflies were playing their last baseball game tonight. "Gee, I sure would like to go to that game," I said. He didn't say anything. I said once again, "Gee, I want to go to the game." He still didn't say anything, so I asked him if he would like to go to the game. "Oh, you want to go to the game?" he asked. I said, "Yes, I do." "Well, I don't have any money," he said. When I told him, I would pay for the tickets, he was okay with going then.

We headed to the stadium. I gave him my keys so he could drive. I paid for the parking when we got there. We went inside and I paid for our tickets at the ticket booth. We found our seats and we were enjoying the game. After a while, I asked him if he was glad he came. He said, "Yes, I really am enjoying it. This is nice."

We were definitely having a good time until he started being disrespectful to me. There was a woman sitting two rows in front of us. She was drinking and she got very loud. Then, she stood up, started shaking her butt, and trying to dance. He couldn't keep quiet. He started egging her on. Every chance he got, he would holler something to her. She came back to where we were sitting and reached across me to high five him. She saw I wasn't laughing. She said, "Mam, you're ready to go home aren't you?" I said, "No, I'm not." She saw the expression on my face and she went back to her seat. We left the game in the middle of the eighth inning. He said he wanted to beat the traffic.

When we got home, he went out on the porch with his cup of liquor as usual. After about an hour, he came inside and started asking me questions about the game I had taken my son to earlier for his birthday. I said, "Yes, we went for his birthday." "When was his birthday and where was I when you went?" he asked. I said, "You know when his birthday is, and I don't know where you were when we went but you weren't home." He asked again, "When is his birthday and why didn't I know y'all were going to a game?" "Like I said, you know his birthdate and I don't know where you were," I told him.

A few minutes later, he asked me when my youngest son's birthdate is. I told him the date. He said, "Oh, so you know his birthdate, but not the other one." I said, "You know both of their birthdates anyway, so I don't know why you are even asking me." He said, "I should have known your stupid ass would say something like that, ignorant ass." "Did you just call me stupid?" I asked. He said, "Yes, damn stupid ass." I didn't say anything else to him. I went upstairs and listened to my Gospel music.

# CHANGING THE LOCKS

## Chapter 13

On November 1, 2016, he left on Tuesday morning about 8:00 a.m. Usually I would take him to Aiken or Augusta, sometimes both, on Tuesdays. I didn't work on Tuesdays. On that day, he didn't even ask me if I wanted to go with him or not. He got in his car and left. When I saw him again, it was Wednesday afternoon.

When he drove up on Wednesday afternoon, I was standing outside on the driveway talking to my daughter on my phone. He parked, got out of his car, and went inside. He didn't even speak to me. A few minutes later, he came back out, got in his car, and left again. Still, he didn't speak to me.

On November 19th, I got sick at work. I was in so much pain I couldn't drive. I called him to come get me. He came, but he had called the paramedics to come too. I was taken to the E.R. After that, I didn't go back to work at all.

On December 19th, he was supposed to go to North Carolina to a Veteran's Facility for 10 weeks. He left on Sunday afternoon on the 18th. A few hours later, I got a call from him. I thought he was calling to tell me he had arrived safely. He actually called me to ask me to come pick him up. He hadn't even left Columbia. He said he had an accident and couldn't drive his car. He also said he had made it to his brother's house and parked. I went to pick him up. Before I left, I asked our daughter if she would drive to North Carolina because I hadn't done much driving since my hospital visit. She said she would take off tomorrow and drive him up there.

In January 2017, our daughter and I went up to visit him. We took some items he needed. On March 3rd, my niece and I went back to bring him home. I drove up and he drove back. After he got home, he waited awhile before he brought his car home. When he finally got it, he parked it in the driveway and seemed to forget about getting it fixed. Later, he said it only needed a tire.

I took him to all his appointments in Hopkins, SC, Aiken, Augusta, and Columbia. I even took him to Wagener on some Tuesday nights for practice. We still had disagreements. There were times when I wouldn't answer him to keep the peace. No matter what he said or did, I was always the one to try to repair the relationship. He would never say he was sorry or wrong about anything.

On April 8th, he went to New York to help his cousin. He was in New York for a week and a half. Therefore, he wasn't home for his birthday on April 12th. I didn't have a problem with that. Even if I had a problem with it, he would have gone anyway.

On May 25th as I was taking him to an appointment in Hopkins, he started accusing me of saying something. He started calling me names. He said I was so stupid and always saying things I knew nothing about. He went on and on. I told him I should stop and put him out of the car. He said, "Put me out of the damn car with your stupid ass self." I said, "I am through with you and the marriage. I don't know what your problem is, but I have had it." He said, "I don't give a damn what you say." I didn't say anything else to him. I took him on to his appointment and waited for him.

On June 1st, while I was taking him to the bank, he started again. He said someone told him I told them about something he had done. I knew what he had done, but I hadn't told anyone about it. He told on himself when he told his psychiatrist about it. He kept saying, "Well, I was told that you told them so and so." He never said who I told because he was lying and trying to find out if I really knew. I told him to go tell whoever told him that I told them that I said, "GO TO HELL!"

On June 6th, our daughter asked him to meet her at Wal-Mart on her lunch break, so she could buy him a tire for his car. I rode with her to Wal-Mart. She told him that was his Father's Day gift. She paid for the tire and we left. Later that afternoon, as our daughter and I were getting ready to go out, he was sitting on the sofa talking on his phone. When he heard our daughter ask me if I was ready, he told the person on the phone he would call them back. He looked at us and said we needed to talk. He started again with the I told somebody that our daughter told me something about something he had done the weekend that I had sat with his sister for her daughter to go out of town story. Yes, I knew what he had done, but I hadn't told anyone. When he said that, I walked on out the door and told our daughter to come on. She stayed inside to hear what he had to say.

When our daughter came out and got in the car, she was angry with me because he had made her think I told him about what happened while I was away at his sister's. Well, that was it for me. I stopped speaking to him. I made up in my mind that if he said anything to me, I would not respond. He told me I had a hearing problem. I ignored that too.

On Tuesday, June 27th, he left home about 6:00 that evening. When I saw him again, it was 5:15 Wednesday evening. We didn't say anything to each other. On Thursday, June 29th, I went to run an errand. When I got back, I saw some mail laying on the couch where I usually sit. When I picked it up, I noticed it was from the mortgage company. He had opened mail that didn't have his name on it. When he came in, I asked him why he opened mail that wasn't his. He said, "I pay the damn bills here. So, I can open anything I want to." I said, "You open some more mail that's not yours and I will let the police know." He started calling me stupid ass. "If I was as stupid as you are, I wouldn't call anyone else stupid," I stated.

On July 3, 2017, I was sitting on the couch watching television when he came out of his bedroom and said he was having the electric transferred. I said, "Oh, are you having it transferred to my name?" He said, "No, I'm having it transferred to my place." I said, "Oh, no problem." My daughter in Virginia had just transferred it to his name a month or two ago. Somehow, she had put all the utilities in her name while I was in Georgia. On July 5th, our daughter and I went to SCE&G and had the electric put in my name. We had to pay the past due bill in order to get it transferred to my name. Two days after he started moving on July 6th, I told him I was changing the locks on the doors since he had moved all his furniture, which was only a bed from my basement and a dresser he had gotten from a friend. He also moved all of his clothes. I didn't want him going in and out when I wasn't there. After I told him I was changing the locks, he stopped moving and left several boxes he had packed in the bedroom and the bathroom. I still changed the locks. Every day after that, he would come by my house and ring the doorbell. When I would go and open the door, it would be him. I knew he was keeping my daughter informed because I heard him a few times on his phone telling her what I was doing. Every day when he came in, he would pretend he was doing something inside, or he would go outside and act as if he was checking the siding on the house.

# MOVING OUT

Chapter 14

On Wednesday, July 12, 2017, the week after he moved out, our daughter and I went to bed that night. When we got up Thursday morning, the water was turned off. We went to the city office where I always paid the bill and asked them why it was turned off. I knew I didn't miss any payments. We were told that my daughter in Virginia requested that it be turned off. I asked if I could have it turned back on if I put the service in my name. The clerk told us that my daughter would have to send a written signed request for them to change it or turn it back on. She suggested we go downtown to the City of Columbia's Water office and talk with someone there.

We went to that office and spoke with a customer service representative. We were told the same thing. The representative said she was so sorry, and she couldn't imagine a daughter having her mother's water turned off. The next day, I texted her and asked if she had the water turned off, and if so, why? She said, "Yes, I had it turned off." I asked her if she would have it turned back on and put it in my name. She said, "No." I asked her, "Why?" She said, "Because you and Tamara are always leaving the house and going somewhere."

He kept on coming by every day, even after she had the water turned off. He knew what she was going to do. I am sure they decided to do that once he had moved. Tamara went to work every day, so she had to be able to shower and I couldn't go around all day and night without a bath. We had to purchase jugs of water and try to bathe that first night.

The second day, I called a friend and asked her if we could live with her until we found a place of our own. I explained to her what happened. She said of course we could come and live with her. She also said she only had one bedroom for us and that if we didn't mind sharing it, we were more than welcome. We moved in with her on Thursday. My daughter in Virginia had the cable turned off that morning.

The next day, Tamara took the day off from work and we went apartment hunting. We looked at nine different places that day. One place waived the first month's rent. It was freshly remodeled, and it was in a very prestigious area. The manager said we wouldn't be able to move in until July 23rd, which was ten days away. We went back to my friend's and told her we wouldn't be able to move in until a week later. She said it was fine and that we could stay as long as we needed to.

Every day that next week, I went to the house and pack some of my belongings. My friend told me every morning before I left her home to take some jugs of water with me. Tamara would come by after work and pack. He would still come by every day and sit there. He would watch television awhile then he would go outside, call my daughter, and tell her what I was doing. He would sneak around and pretend he was measuring the wall or the windows.

The last day we were there, which was Saturday, July 22, we rented a U-Haul. My son came over and helped Tamara and me load it. I gave away most of my furniture, except a few pieces I sold to a furniture storeowner. As the guys were getting the appliances, when they started to get the refrigerator that he had gotten from one of his sisters as a Christmas present for me, he said, "No, don't touch that. It is mine and it's not going anywhere." I said, "You gave me that fridge as a Christmas present." He said, "No, that is mine and it's not going anywhere."

"Mrs. Corley, let's step outside for a moment," the man buying the furniture said. When we got outside, he said, "I could tell you were getting pretty angry and I don't want you to say anything else to him. I see why you are not with him." I said, "Okay, just get the rest of the furniture and the electric range." He had his guys load everything else and they left. He said, "Mrs. Corley, please don't let him upset you too much." I told him I wouldn't.

My son, our daughter, and I finished loading the truck. Before my son left, he said, "Mom, don't even worry about him." I said, "Oh, I won't." When our daughter and I finished and got ready to leave, he was still sitting on the couch. I looked at him and I said, "We are finished and we are leaving. So, you can call my daughter and tell her we are finished so you can stop being her little watch dog." He was so shocked. He opened his mouth but couldn't say anything.

About 6:00 p.m. that evening, my son, our daughter, and I got a group text from my daughter in Virginia. She said that the locks had been changed on the house and if we didn't get that U-Haul off her property, she would have it towed by the police. WOW!! That was one BIG SHOCK!!! Evidently, she was in Columbia all the time as he was watching us. Tamara could see how hurt and upset I was. So, she said, "Mom, I will get my friend that's helping us move tomorrow to go with me to get the truck tonight. You stay here." "Okay, baby," I said. She picked up the young man that was going to help us move the next day and they went and moved the U-Haul down the street from the house.

The next day, which was a Sunday morning, I didn't go back by there with her to get the truck. My friend took her to get it and I waited a few blocks away until she came with the truck. I couldn't bear to see my home for the last time, knowing that I couldn't go on the premises.

Two days after we moved, we got a text from her saying that we had stolen the television remote and that if we didn't return it, she would call the police on Tamara and me. That was it for me! I texted her back and really gave her a piece of my mind. I told her I didn't need it anyway because I had my own. The texts kept coming for the next two days. I just ignored them and deleted them all.

# MY ADVICE

Chapter 15

Well, I wrote all this to say that this was all a part of verbal abuse. He was afraid to physically abuse me because he knew he would have to answer to my son and a couple of my nephews. So, he used his verbal lies to turn my daughter and my great nephew/son against me. Verbal abuse can hurt in so many ways. The longer you put up with it, the worse you will be treated. Get out of the situation before it tears your self-esteem down or cause you to do something that you will regret. There is always a way out. JUST LEAVE!

My daughter and I have left Columbia. I lost a home that was very sentimental to me because my niece, Darline, left it to me in her will. Although she had Multiple Sclerosis, Tamara and I took care of her until her death. Some of my family comes to visit us. My friends keep in touch and continue to pray for us. Some have offered us help with anything we need. We have found a wonderful church that we love attending.

Several friends and family members said they are coming to visit and spend time with us. We are very happy here.

I hope this book will help women and men that have gone through or are going through what I went through. As I said, the scars are on the inside. I didn't want people to know how I was being treated, so I didn't talk about it. I did try to get him to go to counseling with me, but he refused.

There were so many times I sat in church, looking at him singing on the choir and helping conduct praise service. I wanted to scream out and tell people that he was putting on a front, that he had just cursed me out on the way to church. Of course, he played the loving husband when we were in church and around family.

Abused women and men need a support system. We need to know that there is someone or somewhere we can go to get help and to get counseling. We need to stand up for each other. We need someone to talk to. We need to stand up for ourselves and say, "NO MORE!!!"

Although I am out of the relationship, there are still times when I think about it and wonder what I could have done differently. I lost my home, but I didn't lose my self-respect. No one can take that unless you give it.

One piece of advice I would like to offer to anyone reading this book or anyone going through verbal or physical abuse is to get help. Don't let the person abusing you push you to a point of doing something you will regret. Please, talk to someone, get out, and get help. Most importantly, through it all, TRUST IN GOD. Without Him, I don't know what I would have done or where I would be today.

# ABOUT THE AUTHOR

Barbara Corley was born in Lexington, SC. She

graduated from Wagener Salley High School. Her passion for helping others led her to obtain a certificate as a Social Service Assistant from Aiken Technical College. Barbara also received an On Job Training certificate where she will able to help train people within their companies.

Barbara has worked in multiple school districts in South Carolina for 22 years. She has served in a variety of roles as a teacher's assistant, an after school teacher, an in-school suspension monitor, and as a Chapter 1 Tutor providing 10-15 minutes of one-on-one instruction to struggling students.

Barbara enjoys writing. She began writing in her late teens. Her previous work include, Ms. B's Book of Poems. Her upcoming works will include a children's book on friendship and a second book of poems on Love & Faith.

Barbara's passion includes traveling, sewing, and helping others. She makes clothes, draperies, throw pillows, and children's blankets.

Her passion for helping others is evident as she serves as a volunteer in a Rock Hill Church and a counselor and mentor in a Job Corp program for women in women's shelters. She is passionate about ensuring that the older population and the children are taken care of. She believes it is important to help provide them with health care, finances, medical services, or just a friendly talk.

# RESOURCES

**Insights Educational & Treatment Services**
Point of contact – Pansy Anderson
1441 St. Andrews Road
Columbia, South Carolina 29210
(803) 750-8444
www.insightsservices.com

**Verbal Abuse and Therapy**
Point of contact – Patricia Evans
Speaker, Author, and Consultant
Post Office Box 589
Alamo, California 94507
(925) 934-5972
www.verbalabuse.com

**Soul Care Christian Counseling**
Point of contact – Chantelle Johnson, LPC
5501 Executive Center Dr. Suite #238
Charlotte, North Carolina 28212
(980) 613-8312
www.mysoulcare.org

www.ingramcontent.com/pod-product-compliance
Lightning Source LLC
Chambersburg PA
CBHW062028290426
44108CB00025B/2824